In loving memory of our beloved boxer dog Star Star.

Her devotion to our family will always be cherished.

To my husband David, for your unwavering love and support.

To all the children that think they want a duck.

Remember... They poop a lot.

Copyright © 2017 Becky Dembowski

All rights reserved.
No part of this book may be used
or reproduced by any means,
graphic, electronic, or mechanical, including photocopying,
recording or taping or by any information storage retrieval system
without the written permission of the author,
except in the case of brief quotations
embodied in critical articles and reviews.

ISBN : 978-0-9992689-0-2

Editing by Jenny Stinson
Illustrations © 2017 Alicia Young
All original photographs taken by Becky Dembowski

Printed and bound in China
First Printing 2017

* You can see more of Scarlett
and her journey through Facebook and YouTube,
under the author's name.

Scarlett's Journey

The Adventures of a Runner Duck
• Based on a True Story •

Author : Becky Dembowski

Illustrator : Alicia Young

Scarlett was born on a rainy day in April.
She cuddled close to her mom the best she could
while the rain dripped over her downy feathers.
"Be still little one, it's time to sleep," her mama said softly.
When Scarlett became restless and wandered too far from the nest,
she found that she was all alone and getting cold.
Her mother couldn't leave the nest to find her,
because she had other eggs to hatch.
Hearing Scarlett's cry, the farmer's daughter
scooped her up to keep her warm and safe.
Scarlett nestled in a soft blanket and fell fast asleep.
"Mom, can we keep her?" pleaded the farmer's daughter.
As her mom looked at her daughter holding this tiny duckling,
her response was, "Of course, she is now part of our family."

The next morning, Scarlett woke up excited and eager
to begin her journey.

"Be still, little one.
It's time to get ready for the day.
First, let's eat,"
mom whispered.

Scarlett drank her water
and nibbled at her grains,
while chattering.

"When we play outside,
there's sure to be water nearby.
I learned how to blow bubbles today,"
explained Scarlett.

As Scarlett began to feel more comfortable
with her mom, it was time for her
to meet the rest of the family.
Mom introduced her to the curious cat, Tiger;
their old dog Star Star;
and gentle Dorothy, the turkey.

Playing outside was always a treat.
When the kids played hide and go seek,
Scarlett ran to join.

"Scarlett, it's your turn to count,"
explained the children.
"I can't see you.
I'm going to count 1, 2, 3 ... 7, 11, 22,
ready or not, here I come!"
shouted Scarlett.

"Oh boy! Tiger got himself
in BIG trouble," said Scarlett.
"We drove straight to the doctor
to see what was the matter."

"Now be still, Tiger; let the doctor see.
I'll have to hold you down
if you don't stay still,"
bossed Scarlett.

When Scarlett and Tiger
returned from the vet,
Scarlett was playing late outside.

Mom yelled from the house,
"Hurry, run, run! Get off the street.
The policeman is coming;
he might not see you.
RUN, Scarlett, RUN!"

"The next day, Mom asked for my help.
Be still, Star Star; let us help you.
It's okay," soothed Scarlett.

"The medicine will make
your ears feel better.
After, we'll go to lunch."

"Oh look, mom – 'D.'
D is for Duck.
Not just any ordinary duck,
but a special RUNNER DUCK like me."

"I'm a runner duck; I don't fly.
Only the ground for me,"
Scarlett said proudly.

When the farmer's daughter
went to the dentist,
Scarlett was right beside her.

"Hold still, sister, so the dentist
can see your teeth."

"Mom, when is it my turn? Oh, but wait.
I don't have any teeth,"
Scarlett remembered.

As she grew, Scarlett loved car rides,
bananas, grapes,
and everything to do with water.

"What an adventure this will be!
Car rides are my favorite.
Let's GO!"

"Be still, little one," Daddy explained.
"You can ride as long as you don't poop
in my new 1964 Bonneville Station Wagon."

"Doesn't he know I can't hold it?"
Scarlett wondered.

Scarlett continued to grow bigger every day,
but she still loved to take naps,
especially with Dorothy.

"Shhhh, Dorothy. Let's take a nap.
I know you love it when
I sing you to sleep," Scarlett whispered.

"Hmmm, hmm," Scarlett hummed.

Scarlett continued to grow bigger every day,
but she still loved to take naps,
especially with Dorothy.

"Shhhh, Dorothy. Let's take a nap.
I know you love it when
I sing you to sleep," Scarlett whispered.

"Hmmm, hmm," Scarlett hummed.

When Scarlett grew up,
she met other runner ducks
who were just like her.
She became good friends with them,
mostly Jake, because he was
the same age as her.

Jake liked to explore
with Scarlett in the yard,
looking for bugs in the water.

Finally, the day came
when it was time to live
with the other runner ducks.

"Be still, mom, it's time for me to go.
I'm all grown up now,"
Scarlett said as she rested her head
gently over her mom's shoulder.

"You took good care of me,
and now it's time for me to go."

"I'll always love you."

The
journey
continues...

This Book Belongs to:

_____

What I like best about Scarlett:

_____

Where my next adventure will be:

_____

www.ingramcontent.com/pod-product-compliance
Lightning Source LLC
Chambersburg PA
CBHW042019090426
42811CB00015B/1685